Dopamine Clouds Over Knighton Park

I0117872

Philip Hill

chipmunkapublishing
the mental health publisher

Philip Hill

Published by
Chipmunkapublishing
PO Box 6872
Brentwood
Essex CM13 1ZT
United Kingdom

http://www.chipmunkapublishing.com

Edited by Michelle Karpus

Chipmunkapublishing gratefully acknowledge the support of Arts Council England.

About The Author

Philip Hill has spent most of his life living in various parts of Birmingham. Philip is a twin and his twin brother Paul is a neighbour. Furthermore Philip has an elder sister and an elder brother he has not seen recently.

Being brought up with his twin brother and adopted sister Lynn by foster parents gave him much needed stability after living in a children's home. Experiencing neglect in a children's home at the early stages of development led to him being sent to a special school at the age of five. He learned to read by the age of ten and eventually went on to Leicester University to study Economics.

At Leicester University Philip struggled with mixing with his peer group and despite reasonable academic progress had a nervous breakdown after passing his finals. His diagnosis of Schizophrenia would be a label he will now have to endure for the rest of his life.

After having a relapse Philip eventually found long term work. Then at the age of 32 Philip went to Birmingham University where he gained a masters degree in Economic Development and Policy. He then went on to study for a doctorate but ended up with the consolation prize of a Masters of Philosophy research degree. Finally drawing on his skills as a support worker working with those diagnosed with mental health issues, he applied to go on a social work course. Philip is now a professional social worker working with adults with learning disabilities. He is also happily married to Geraldine.

CHAPTER ONE – THE PSYCHOTIC EXPERIENCE

A tall, six foot skinny underweight man with thick overgrown hair was tossing and turning in his sleep. The sheets had not been washed for months and a stale odour pervaded his small cramped room. He had a sickly white complexion which had allowed his stubble to become overgrown as well as his nails. This man was Aiden, or Ade to his friends, and he had reached a crisis in his life.

Aiden was an Economic History student at Lanchester University and his room was part of the Elm Tree Road student's accommodation complex. He had always been seen by some of his fellow students as a bit of a 'loner' and a 'misfit'. He had previously worn a battered parker raincoat on campus with flares and a knitted pullover until one student dared to call him 'reindeer man.' He had been perceived by some students as behaving rather oddly and had an eccentric, overly energetic dance style at the weekly student 'Mega Disco.' He had also been known for a bombastic taste in music and had inflicted various dramatic classical music pieces on his fellow students from his tape player in his room.

Students at Pollage hall had felt he had been pursuing a small attractive student called Janice over the previous twelve months and seemed incorrigible and undaunted by repeated rejections.

Over the month of June 1987 his behaviour had become more and more bizarre. He had stormed down to Pollage hall where he felt Janice lived and delivered an angry letter at her refusal not only to engage with him but to engage in public displays of affection with her blonde rugby boyfriend Dean.

However on the 30th of June things got out of control.

Dopamine Clouds Over Knighton Park

As he began to think about the symptoms of sleeplessness he had experienced, Aiden started to get psychotic thoughts.

He had been trying to lie down and sleep but he kept getting up all the time. He was fixated with Janice and what she might be saying to him.

For the previous 18 months he had been trying to imagine how Janice would respond to his change of image. His new clothes and haircut had failed so far to initiate a response from her. He had tried so hard to imagine what she was thinking over such a long time. Then one night in a frenzied anxious state he finally managed to get inside her head.

Rather than second guessing what was drifting about in Janice's mind, he finally felt he knew. But it was not just Janice.

Aiden really felt now that he listened in on the thoughts of all his friends and Janice's mates as well. While such thought dialogue was positive about him this did not matter. But tonight it did matter. It seemed now that everyone had turned on him.

He sensed Janice's fear but he also sensed a growing sense of her antagonism towards him. He had a sense of being flirted at or toyed with. This began to make him feel angry. He had started out twenty minutes earlier by imagining what Janice was thinking. Now he knew. And within moments he sensed that she had told all his friends at the University and even at the Athletics club in Birmingham about what had been up to over the previous eighteen months.

The only solution, he recalled to these persistent and intensifying thought patterns, seemed to be to go where the source of these voices were coming from. This meant he remembered going to where he felt she lived and confronting her there. He walked up Elm Tree Road and he felt eerie. He was now inhabiting a strange world. He felt that he knew what she was thinking; everyone knew his history to a point that the first person he recalled seeing gave a rather knowing stare. It was now six am in the morning.

Even the roads signs he could see had a particular meaning that was a preparation for him at that moment in time. They seemed to be warning him against any wayward behaviour.

As he approached Pollage hall he had felt for some reason that it must be a block where she lived and so he began a process of knocking on each door.

Recounting this event later to himself many years later he remembered how increasingly desperate it made him feel. After a few anguished responses from the few people that did answer their doors, Aiden banged his fists on the floor whilst kneeling down and planned how he was going to throw himself under the next oncoming vehicle on

Knighton Road. This really seemed the end for Aiden. With no Janice there was no future. He might as well just die because everything else felt futile.

His thoughts were interrupted by a distant shout he could hear down the corridor. It was the voice of a middle aged bearded man. He introduced himself as the Pollage Hall Warden and asked him to leave because he was causing a nuisance. Then on the way downstairs he asked him if he needed any help and after reflecting on the fact that moments earlier he was planning how he was going to throw myself under a vehicle he said an emphatic yes.

Aiden was given a lift to the student health centre by the warden an hour later. The warden commented, after a time spent with his wife and children getting ready for school, that the colour had started to return to his cheeks.

Dopamine Clouds Over Knighton Park

The college warden drove up the road round Knighton Park to the Student Health Centre. On arrival he was introduced to the duty doctor. He was a bearded man wore a white turban with a grey suite and tie.

The Sikh doctor asked him how he was feeling. He told him. "I'm mad aren't I?"

Then in a patronizing manner the G.P said, "I suppose we're all mad."

Aiden kept drifting in and out of psychosis and felt that the suggestive, almost leading, questioning of the Asian doctor's assessment almost hypnotically drew him back into psychosis.

He remembered feeling a sudden elevation in status. Perhaps 'The Guardian' headlines were directly addressed at him after all. The articles about nuclear weapons were warning him of a long awaited apocalypse and he had been ignoring his calling to warn the world of such a catastrophe. The time had now come indeed it was my time to follow in the footsteps of Jesus and offer the world a prophesy.

Before he was able to get deeply into a prophetic mode he recalled being left in the company of a nurse. In the background he could hear the news headlines. But these were no ordinary headlines; they seemed to be addressed at him and his new prophetic role. He then was ashamed of what he did next as he began to ape the behaviour of a small child and began eating items off the nurse's plate without invitation which shocked the nurse momentarily.

Then the ambulance came and as it did he was now thinking about how he felt his long term destiny had been to join the navy as an engineering officer. He began to think about what Janice might think of that and as he did he thought of the ambulance as part of a journey to a transformative experience to achieve this. Then he had this negative vibe come all over him as he realized that Janice might still reject me after this transformation and he began to weep.

After a journey lasting ten minutes Aiden arrived at Lanchester General Hospital and upon entering the hospital became confused when a woman called Maria asked his name.

He remembered how humiliated he felt when he said in response to the question 'what is your name?'
"Aiden... no... Earth Andrew," at which she burst into ridicule.

Upon arrival at the hospital he composed himself and after going through the entrance he walked into the television lounge. He switched over television channels at random in a lounge which had had a captive audience. Each program caused his thoughts to become disturbed until he chanced upon the BBC's Wimbledon coverage.

A player called Pernfors was playing an ageing but legendary Jimmy Connors.

Aiden remembered that all the things that he was uncertain of in his world were allied to the forces that accompanied Pernfors whereas all the forces of certainty were with Connors. He had been willing Jimmy Connors to win before he was interrupted by a visitor. It was the social worker.

Aiden told the social worker that he thought for some reason his mother was dead. The social worker assured him his mother was not dead. However he could not remember much more of that conversation taking medication the nurses had given him.

The next thing he knew he was getting up at about 8 in the morning. He tried to sense once more how he had felt. It had taken about a minute before he was orientated to time and place and remembered what had happened the day before. The psychotic thoughts seemed to have gone and there was no trauma. Then as he tried to get out of bed he remembered that he had been given medication. He felt really old as each moment passed he became aware of agonizingly slow the whole bodily movement was.

After breakfast Aiden tried to read the newspapers but after a couple of sentences would drift asleep.

Was this sedation the price he would have to pay from now on for sane thoughts? Was it a waste of time getting a degree if he ended up like a zombiefied vegetable? Would he find a long term companion to share his life? To these questions the nurses gave non committal responses.

It had been a strange other worldly experience he had been through that had no name. It was three months before to find out that his condition would need to be stabilized on a long term basis and that the name for this life changing experience was Schizophrenia. Aiden remembered meeting a former friend twelve months previously who had the same diagnosis. There was a vivid recall of how frightened and uncomfortable it had made had feel. Now he wondered how people would react to him. Not only was this a so called condition but it had a label that would stay with him for the rest of his life.

It was as though his life had come to pre-mature end.

CHAPTER TWO – 'BRIEF ENCOUNTER'
THIRTEEN YEARS LATER

Aiden was on the 6.55 train from Waterloo heading to Lee station. It was dusk on a late August evening in 1999 and he was in the company of his friend Andy whom he was visiting from Birmingham for a weekend. Andy had put him up for the night when he ran the London marathon six years earlier. Aiden was now a doctoral student attending Birmingham University. He was now six stone heavier with a large build and sporting a dark ginger beard and a protruding belly.

Things had turned out well considering that twelve years earlier he had been diagnosed with Paranoid Schizophrenia. He had spent five years working for the National Schizophrenia Fellowship helping fellow sufferers and now he was working on a research project to understand what would help them find and retain employment as well as thrive in a job. He was struggling with another affair of the heart and it had been three years since he had finally rid himself of an emotional attachment to Janice.

Aiden looked out of the corner of his eye and he could see a familiar pink jacket. He had been arguing about the excessive fast pace of that day's whistle stop tour with Andy when he stopped mid conversation and said he had recognized someone he thought he knew and then went to investigate.

As he approached closer to the woman in the pink felt coat he felt more and more certain it was Janice until when ten yards away he had the confidence to say, "I believe you graduated from Lanchester University in 1987 in Economics."

She said, "Yes."

He then enquired. "How are you doing?"

"I stayed on at Lanchester and did a Masters Degree in Economic Development and Policy."

He interjected. "That's a coincidence I went to Birmingham to do the same Masters nine years later."

"What are you doing now?" she asked.

"I'm doing a doctorate in Social Policy finding out how people with mental health issues can find and keep a job."

She then started to explain how she had worked at a Japanese Stockbrokers in London for seven years before starting work as an IT specialist at Greenwich University.

Aiden then asked if she knew Michael Oliver.

"I can't recall that name," she exclaimed.

Aiden then explained how Michael Oliver was one of the country's leading experts on the social model of disability and is based at Greenwich University. When describing his own research as working with fellow disabled people he saw her scowl. It was as though Aiden was not good enough to be deserved to have a disability. She seemed to hint Schizophrenia was not a disability it was a disease of the mind.

When he said it was good for fellow friends to be reunited he saw an irritated expression on her face. Aiden recognized this was an acquaintance where he had tried to force a friendship and inside his head he winced at the use of this f word in her presence.

Feeling he had nothing more to say Aiden said goodbye and rejoined Andy across the other side of the carriage.

Aiden realized with the management of that encounter how much he had moved on. Then he started to reminisce about the crisis he had had with Janice thirteen years before.

CHAPTER THREE – THIRTEEN YEARS EARLIER

Aiden was a troubled soul. Ever since he had moved into a self catering hall at Lanchester University he had begun to question whether he was normal.

It was his flat mate who had first planted the seeds of doubt in his head. It had been quite easy to come home and study at Villa Hall where Julian, a recluse, had never bothered him. Now in Mary Dee residences Shane kept putting the Duran single *planet earth* on repeat to an extent where he couldn't hear himself think. He kept asking himself whether he was a 'square' challenging Shane to turn the music down. All the other students seemed to be into his type of music, so why not him?

There had been another reason why Aiden had begun to doubt his sanity.

Dopamine Clouds Over Knighton Park

He had met this woman during the first lecture of the New Year. She was a petite brunette freckled lady. She was later to be seen sporting a pink overcoat. She had been extremely friendly. Her name was Janice.

He had asked a guy in front of him about the lecture on Macro-economics and Janice had interjected smiling as she did so. It seemed she was quite nosey as it turned out. Aiden was quite overwhelmed and flattered by the attention. He left the lecture theatre feeling that it was a one off encounter and that was all. However a week later when leaving the same scheduled lecture he looked up as he ascended the stairs from the Atomborough lecture Theatre and as he did his eyes met Janices' as she walked from the top of the stair case to the entrance. She gave a delirious smile and it was at that exact moment that he fell in love.

Aiden had never properly been in love before and now he felt that Janice really liked him too.

About two days later Aiden happened to chance upon Janice in the newsagents of the Student Union building.
'Hello,' he said, nervously.

'Hi,' she replied.

After some introductory pleasantries, she asked, 'Do you know anyone from Lanchester University Rugby club?' He was only to find out the significance of the question eighteen months later and by then everyone else was questioning his sanity.

As they exchanged their farewells by the entrance to the student's union building Aiden tried to make the most of the opportunity and asked if Janice would consider going out with him in future. She rather hurriedly agreed and like a rabbit caught in headlights she made a panicky move for the exit to the building.

Aiden was elated and he could not wait for the next opportunity of the next macro- economics lecture to meet her again. He was even awake for a few hours late at night at the exciting prospect of meeting her again.

When the day for the lecture came Aiden sat at the back of the lecture theatre in his usual spot. At the end of the lecture Janet made a hurried rush for the exit and it wasn't until leaving the Atomborough building that Aiden caught up with her. She saw him and her response was to shield her face under her coat as she ran away from him into the student's union building.

Aiden stood motionless and in deep shock at the impact of what had happened had just sunk in. He couldn't believe that someone would humiliate him like this. He asked himself whether or not he was a bad enough person to be treated like this. And as he did so he became rather angry. He felt he had been just been made to feel a freak and he didn't deserve that. Then he regained his composure and went into the building Janice had entered moments earlier determined to confront her.

After searching the student's union shop and the outside of Queen's Hall he descended the stairs and saw her from a distance surrounded by friends. Her face sunk into her coat. A guy in a cream coloured mackintosh walked towards him and told him that Janice had considered going out with him but that she had decided to stick with her boyfriend. Aiden did not believe this excuse and instead wondered why she did not have the courage to explain this to him herself.

Aiden walked slowly back to his flat in a resigned and angry mood.
He did not know yet but he would not move on from these feelings of loss and rejection for decades.

After the initial rejection by Janice, Aiden decided he would not talk to her and would ignore her if he saw her on campus.

However when he did see her about a week later in Queen's Hall she uttered a hello to him and he found himself not knowing what to do. He then replied hello and left the building.

These mixed up and confused feelings were to demonstrate themselves in the form of contradictory behaviour. For example one day that winter he walked across the snow strewn Victoria Park and saw Janice but this time decided to ignore her. On another occasion he approached her in the library and started up a conversation.

For a couple of weeks during lunch breaks he found himself just going down to the bar, where Janice was, and playing the pinball machines from a discrete distance. However, despite agonizing with himself he could not go over and talk to her.

He now had to admit to himself that he still loved Janice. The strategy now was to go about his everyday business but to conduct an image change. This would hopefully get back to Janice and he would somehow force her to re-evaluate him so that they could at least be friends.

The image change should be radical so that it was noticed. A shorter tidier haircut would be a starting point. Wearing grey colours would also be the new normal colour for him. His taste in music would change as the middle of the road sounds of new wave were dispensed with in favour of classical music. It was not long before the sounds of Beethoven were resonating from his room.

Weekly visits to the 'Mega Disco' were part of the attempt to win back Janice. But what should have been a casual night out ended up with frantic dancing styles that sent out a message of desperation rather than coolness.

When it became apparent after eighteen months that these strategies were no longer working, a crisis set in. The end of the finals and the imminent journey to live back with his parents filled Aiden with dread.

Aiden began to feel that Janet and her friends were against him and worse than that he began to believe they were discrediting him to other people that were important in his life.

Within months he was resident at the Mental Health wing of Lanchester General Hospital.

CHAPTER FOUR – REQUESTING THERAPY SESSIONS

Aiden had spoken to his psychiatrist. Membi was a black African from Nigeria. By the time of the meeting he had known Aiden for five years. Aiden posed a question in his consultation session. He wondered whether Janice lived in Birmingham. It had been seven years since he had first met her. He wondered what the chances were of meeting her again. He felt he may have seen her at an orchestral concert in the Symphony Hall. The psychiatrist frowned.

"What are the odds of meeting her again do you think?"

Aiden replied, "Twenty five to one."

"I think your odds may be a bit short," he said.

Aiden then said that he felt he had not moved on at all since being at Lanchester with his breakdown in the late eighties. He then asked whether he could have therapy. He went on to explain that since having his medication lowered he was more in touch with his feelings. It was therefore an ideal time to explore them and see if he could possibly move on.

Aiden was still on depot injections at this stage. In effect what kept him sane was a monthly dose of 60 milligram's of Flupenthixol Decoanate. This was transferred to his body by a large needle prodded into the large muscle groups in his buttocks. The medication was encased in coconut oil and insertion in the muscles would allow the slow release of this anti-psychotic serum to be gradually released into the bloodstream over the period of a month by which time it was time for another needle.

Aiden's experience of this medication was to feel zonked out for about five days, to feel okay for a fortnight and then to feel increasingly anxious as the time neared for the next injection.

The psychiatrist had warned him that there could be a long wait for a therapist.

So when Aiden found himself sitting in front of a therapist, whose name was Mary, after six weeks, he was pleasantly surprised.

CHAPTER FIVE – DEALING WITH THE LABEL

There had been seven years since last seeing Janice but still Aiden yearned for her. He would go to classical music concerts regularly and see a person in the distance and hope it was her. It was quite clear he had not moved on.

He had ended his first session of therapy getting quite emotional with Mary.

It had been a huge task to go through the most distressing period of his life to a relative stranger. He was also coming to terms with his diagnosis and the negative associations it had for other people. He often thought about other famous people such as Jack the Ripper and Syd Barrett of Pink Floyd who had had a similar diagnosis to him. When he read the latest tabloid headline about a so called 'maniac' or 'nutter' he felt he had more in common with a *psychotic alien species* than to the human race.

Another service user had told him that being diagnosed with Paranoid Schizophrenia was like being diagnosed with cancer.

When he told people, whether they were friends or employers about having schizophrenia he could visibly see their faces tighten as the news sunk in. From being told he was overqualified for a position to people expressing concern about how he would cope with the stress of work.

Still he had done something that ninety per cent of people with his diagnosis had not managed; he had got a job albeit in a nursing home. It had taken him nearly fifty interviews over two years to reassure employers that he could be trusted as an employee. Technically he had done this by lying about his illness until he had gained sufficient experience for his diagnosis to be ignored. In his latest job he felt that a lived experience of mental illness would help him to identify with clients and fortunately his employer took that view too.

He was now working with people with mental health issues at Larchmere Nursing home. The difference with him was that these people were unlucky enough to be treated in the days before community care. They had simply been left on the ward to stagnate for years and years. Aiden knew his heritage and his history and understood how difficult it was before the advent of advanced medication for so called psychiatric patients to escape the asylum.

He had remembered when he was in hospital how difficult it had been to see a plaque on which was inscribed:

THIS PLAQUE IS IN MEMORY OF BOB SMITH

WHO SPENT 44 YEARS OF HIS LIFE IN THIS HOSPITAL

He was appalled at the waste of someone's life.

A local hospital had been closed and many of the patients on the long stay wards had been transferred to the nursing home where he was now working.

He could see these people had been neglected for many years and many seemed so zonked up with medication and had institutionalized practices it was obvious to even a neutral observer that they were very needy, dependent and visibly damaged in their mannerisms.

He was going in to help them in the nursing home but really this was a back water place and little more than a hospital in the community. Residents were given little more than medication and left to amuse themselves in front of the television. He spoke to one of the staff, Lindsey, who had arranged to have a four page version of his illness experience. She, a small woman with a soothing voice, was the caring sort and was one of the better members of staff.

'My daughter read your story as she was typing it up and feels it could be turned into a book.' You ought to try and get this published,' she said enthusiastically. It would really help other people.

But Aiden replied that it was merely preparation for his next session of therapy.

CHAPTER SIX – RECALLING FURTHER PAINFUL MEMORIES

There had been a steady realization that much of the dialogue between Aiden and his therapist was effectively one way traffic with Mary asking the odd question to clarify what was being said. The first couple of sessions were going to be like this with Mary taking brief notes. She said she would only start intervention on the third session.

The second session was less about telling a story but more about trying to be understood. Aiden had some clear theories about why he had been unable to cope as a student.

He explained to Mary that much of his childhood had been so controlled it had felt like a prison. He had been bought up by a mother who had later been diagnosed with obsessive compulsive disorder.

Dopamine Clouds Over Knighton Park

Much of the way she ran his life was very regimented. From the time he got up to the time he went to bed every decision had been made for him. From the breakfast he ate, the clothes he wore, the food he ate, the programmes he watched, the toys he played with; everything was very strictly controlled. As a young child this felt okay but as he grew older he compared experiences with people at school and found out there were less restrictive styles of parenting out there.

He had come home from school as a teenager only to be told to strip wash without privacy and then get changed into his pajamas before eating sandwiches, doing homework and going to bed at eight o'clock just after Coronation Street. There was little room in this regime for mixing with peers. He had never had a girlfriend let alone a girl he could call a friend. Reading books, collecting stamps and building Lego were the less messy activities that were more acceptable and all of these activities took place in the kitchen under he watchful eye of mother, whose name was Jane.

Aiden recalled he had never had much freedom. He could barely concentrate on reading because the radio was on all the time and he wasn't allowed the privacy of going to a room on his own to read. On the rare occasions he was allowed upstairs during the day it was to do homework in a chilly environment with no heating.

He remembered vividly the time when he was threatened to be beaten with a large stick and the time he was thrown to the floor in anger. Aiden could not show his true feelings. If he did he would get into trouble. And so over the years Aiden learned to deny his true feelings to a point where as an older person he became emotionally illiterate.

In the regime there were unwritten rules which once broken led to threats like, 'you're not too big to be hit,' and 'children should be seen and not heard.'

Much of the time if rules were unbroken nothing was said. In fact there were eerie silences fearful of something incurring her wrath but deeply hurtful things were said should her wrath be incurred. Aiden recalled Jane's favourite phrases which included 'your eyes are bigger than your belly'; you're selfish and all you think about is number one.'

All these events had led to coming home from school and having to retreat in a shell. These were not the conditions under which Aiden was going to develop any emotional coping strategies for later in life let alone University. To survive in such a controlled, claustrophobic environment involved Aiden suppressing his own feelings to a point where he became good at going along with others without giving himself permission to ask how he felt.

Aiden told Mary that this lack of emotional literacy led him to be in denial for eighteen months during his first emotional crisis. The second session had been different for Aiden and apart from questions to clarify detail Aiden had not only told the story of his childhood he had begun to self analyse and self criticize again, just as he had done when he had been a student.

Finally as the hour duration approached Mary put her pen down and said that the first couple of sessions would be the material on which the therapy was based and arranged a meeting for three weeks later.

Talking to Mary over the next ten years Aiden revealed situations in which he would have crushes on women which then became affairs of the heart. Each time he would agonise over the pain that this caused. In the end the only way he could cope was to blurt out his feelings to the person concerned. Humiliation and rejection would follow. However each successive time this happened he would recover a bit more quickly in the process.

Towards the end of this decade of therapy the therapist would hint that Aiden had reached the emotional age of his peers. Aiden was now therefore a well adjusted man in his mid thirties.

CHAPTER SEVEN – THE THERAPISTS ANALYSIS

The therapist, Mary, was a large African-Carribean woman who didn't give much away with her facial expressions. She paused for a moment before she began to talk.

Aiden said, 'I'm not much into the medical explanation of my diagnosis.'

'Neither am I, but don't tell anyone otherwise I will get into trouble,' replied Mary.

Then she said that what she was offering me was Cognitive Behavioural Therapy.

She stated that she was going to offer Aiden tools which he could then use to transform his thoughts and then change his behaviour.

Mary said, 'the problem seems to be that you only have conditional self regard for yourself. This means you can only feel positive about yourself when a woman you are attracted to gives you emotional warmth that you lacked in your childhood. The aim of this therapy is to get you to a point of unconditional self regard when you can find these positive feelings within yourself.'

Aiden stated that much of how he thought about himself had been dependent on Janice but that he had some success in generating his own feeling of self worth.

However one of the sessions started really badly. Aiden explained that some students had referred to him as a 'misfit.' Mary was in a philosophical mood and said, 'what's wrong with that, the actual meaning of the word is quite harmless?' But as she said that she realized she had misjudged Aiden who began to sob uncontrollably.

Aiden explained that he had done a great deal to fit in with his peers since his illness and that the term by which he was often referred to was no longer useful.

Mary admitted she had made a mistake and used the rest of that session to build Aiden's confidence.

Aiden would sit there for another nine years as he put his hang ups over Janice and other women through close examination. He felt a need to joke around at the end of each session to de-stress himself of the previous hour's conversation. At the end of it all he felt he understood his feelings more but didn't know whether he had the skills or stamina to deal with his emotions should he encounter someone for which the earth moved.

CHAPTER EIGHT – MOVING BEYOND THE LABEL

Aiden was celebrating his forty-second birthday. There didn't seem cause to celebrate. He was reflecting on the pinnacle he had reached. Yet reaching those dizzy heights didn't necessarily make him a happy man.

He had now passed his probationary period as a social worker a titanic feat for someone still taking medication to ward off a psychotic illness.

He had had offers to be a role model for other disabled people especially mental health survivors yet had declined participating in a television documentary. He didn't want to become the world's expert on Schizophrenia, he wanted to be normal.

Yet normality meant taking on the responsibility of a stressful job and being expected to learn, develop and grow from experience. He could not blame his illness for his mistakes now. The standards of professional behaviour he was now meant to uphold were also very high. He felt on top of a tall building and being frightened it was going to topple at any moment.

He remembered texting his old friend Nikki once about how he had suicidal feelings but was sensible enough to take her advice and take a month out of work. He had learned since then to emotionally distance, to some extent, from his work.

In his re registration document to the General Social Care Council his manager Glady's had put that he was an effectual social worker who managed his mental health at work really well.

Being a very chaotic person Aiden found the daily routine ground him down.

He had learned from his limited experience some very good coping strategies at work. Aiden hated open plan and could feel at times that people, particularly managers, were talking about him. He had learned the art of approaching people and asking them whether he had been the topic of conversation and to accept their response at face value.

Aiden learned that his hang ups over women would be a life time problem and that like most recovering alcoholics he had to talk about recovery over a lifetime. However he now understood his illness and the insecurities that fed it. He was now able to relate to a peer group and encounter many of his daily struggles like most of his contemporaries. It had been a twenty year journey but he had, with the help of his friends and some professionals, got there.